JOAN LAY'S BOOK OF SALADS

Joan Lay's
BOOK OF SALADS

by

JOAN LAY
N.D., M.B.N.O.A.

Drawings by Graham Lester

THORSONS PUBLISHERS LIMITED
Wellingborough, Northamptonshire

First published 1976

ISBN 0 7225 0289 3

Typeset by Specialised Offset Services Ltd., Liverpool
and printed by Whitstable Litho Ltd., Whitstable, Kent

CONTENTS

Except where marked, the ingredients in the recipes are sufficient to serve four, but quantities can of course be varied.

It is more satisfactory to make up your own salad dressings, and recipes for those mentioned can be found at the back of the book.

INTRODUCTION

There are so many different types of salads and vegetables available today that no salad meal need ever be dull or criticized on the grounds that it is 'the same old thing'. Up to eight or nine basic ingredients will be adequate if alternated with simpler combinations; too many mixtures can be indigestible and also rather expensive. Experimentation is the keyword, and even those with little time to spare will be able to produce attractive and appetizing salads. The basic requirement is something on which to build, and this usually comprises lettuce, watercress, mustard and cress, or endive; additional ingredients are then put with it, or piled on it, as the case may be.

The importances of eating some raw food every day cannot be over-emphasized. Everyone knows the value and necessity of vitamins and mineral salts in the diet; and what better way is there of providing them than in salads? There is, however, something more in raw foods than their component parts, and this 'something' is growth vitality, derived from earth and sun. This is why freshness is all-important.

Ideally food should be taken from the garden to the table in a matter of hours. The longer the delay between cutting (or picking) and serving, the greater the loss of vitality in vitamins and minerals. Those who have their own gardens, or who live within easy reach of shops selling fresh produce are fortunate; but those having to rely on supermarkets must do the best they can by using the salads and vegetables immediately, refraining from harming them further by prolonged soaking in water, or by cutting them up a long time before they are needed.

Salad greens should be handled with care as bruised parts cannot crispen; it is always better to tear lettuce than to cut it, because cutting causes a much heavier 'bleeding' of the essential juices. Initially, salads should be washed under running water (not too forcefully), drained well and dried, either by gentle shaking in a salad basket, or in a tea towel. After placing the salad in a polythene bag it should be left in the salad drawer – or low down in the fridge – for a few minutes.

It is difficult to make a salad look unattractive; but there are degrees of appeal, and a little more time spent arranging the salad stuffs and considering contrast is well worth while. Children especially react to shape and colour, and it helps to encourage them to see how many of the ingredients they can recognize. Some children seem to dislike salads, but they can be tempted with stuffed tomatoes, rice and vegetable salads, after which the basic green varieties can be introduced gradually.

The variety of salad stuffs is far greater than one might at first suppose. All root vegetables can be included raw, except perhaps potato, which is rather insipid. Celeriac is a great standby, while turnips, parsnips – even swedes – can be included in small amounts, after being grated fairly finely. All the herbs can be used in turn, then there are young dandelion leaves, nasturtium leaves and sorrel. Less usual vegetables are salsify, seakale, kohl rabi, fennel root and leaf, peppers, red cabbage, and so on. If fruits are also used one begins to appreciate the wide range of possible variations.

Try some of them; and good eating to you!

HORS D'OEUVRE and PARTY PIECES

In this section certain combinations of salads and fruits are given in small quantities and can be served either as *hors d'oeuvre*, or buffet dishes, or snacks at a buffet party. Two or three can be combined to make a main salad. Try them out for yourself.

AVOCADO, APPLE AND WALNUT

$\frac{1}{2}$ Avocado per person
$\frac{1}{2}$ Apple per person
6 half Walnuts per person
Lemon and Honey dressing, or French dressing, or Yogurt or natural dressing

Halve and de-stone avocados; peel, core and dice the apples, chop the walnuts, and combine in the dressing of your choice, then pile into the hollows of the avocados.

AVOCADO AND TINNED APRICOTS WITH WATERCRESS

1 small tin of Apricots
$\frac{1}{2}$ Avocado per person
1 bunch of Watercress
French dressing, or Lemon and Honey dressing

Drain the tin of apricots, cut the halves in half again and pile onto the halved and stoned avocados. Roughly chop the washed and dried watercress and garnish generously, add French dressing, or lemon and honey dressing.

AVOCADO AND CHESTNUTS

4 to 5 Chestnuts per person
$\frac{1}{2}$ Avocado per person
French dressing

Use either fresh, dried or tinned chestnuts (the latter will need no preparation) allowing 4 to 5 chestnuts to each half avocado. Dried chestnuts will need to be simmered gently until soft, then cooled, while fresh chestnuts will need boiling for 15 to 20 minutes so that they can be skinned when cool. Having prepared the chestnuts, just toss in French dressing and fill avocado hollows.

CELERY, PEAR AND WALNUT

1 head of Celery
2 Pears (Comice or William)
4 oz. (115g) Walnuts
French dressing, Yogurt dressing or Mayonnaise

Scrub and dry celery, removing the coarser sticks (these can be kept for soup or stockpot); peel pears and quarter them, removing cores. Chop celery very finely, dice the pears, coarsely chop the walnuts, and combine together in French dressing, yogurt dressing or mayonnaise. Serve on individual dishes or plates on a nest of lettuce, or cress, or endive. Or, leave in a bowl for guests to help themselves.

PINEAPPLE, PEAR AND COTTAGE CHEESE

1 small fresh Pineapple
8 oz. (230g) Cottage Cheese
2 to 3 Pears as to size

Peel pineapple, removing all the eyes, and chop fairly small. Put cottage cheese into a mixing bowl, add the chopped pineapple and mix well. Peel, core and dice the pears, and add these to the mixture. Serve in individual bowls with a slice of tomato or a sprig of parsley as garnish. No dressing needed, but a shake of black pepper and a pinch of sea salt may be added.

PINEAPPLE, HAZELNUT AND BANANA

1 small fresh Pineapple
4 to 6 oz. (115 to 170g) Hazelnuts
2 Bananas

Peel pineapple and cut into small pieces; roughly chop hazelnuts and peel and slice bananas; mix pineapple, hazelnuts and bananas with dressing of your choice, and serve with sprigs of watercress.

Note: Cream cheese diluted with milk (about a tablespoonful) and beaten with a teaspoonful soft brown sugar makes a good dressing for this salad.

WATERCRESS, NUTMEAT AND CARROT

1 bunch of Watercress
1 tin of Nutmeat
2 large Carrots
Onion rings to garnish
French dressing

Wash and drain watercress; grate carrot and mix with French dressing. Put carrot mixture onto individual plates, and surround with a ring of watercress. Dice the nutmeat and arrange on the cress. Garnish with onion rings.

BEETROOT AND CELERY

3 to 4 small Beetroots
1 head of Celery
2 tablespoonsful of Mayonnaise
Parsley sprigs or Green Olives

Cook and dice beetroot; scrub and dry celery, removing the coarser sticks (these can be kept for soup or stockpot), and chop finely, add diced beetroot and mayonnaise and combine together – all will go pink. Serve in dishes and garnish with parsley or green olives.

COTTAGE CHEESE, APPLE, CARROT AND RAISINS

8 oz. (230g) Cottage Cheese
1 Carrot
1 Apple
3 tablespoonsful dried Raisins
chopped Nuts to garnish

Grate carrot and apple, and wash and dry raisins; put cottage cheese into a mixing bowl and add raisins (if cheese is stiff add a tablespoonful of milk or yogurt) add grated carrot and apple and stir in immediately to prevent oxidization. No dressing is necessary, but a shake of freshly ground black pepper and sea salt may be needed according to taste. Serve in glasses and sprinkle with chopped nuts.

DANDELION LEAVES, APPLE AND BANANA

3 to 4 Dandelion leaves per person
(or as a substitute 2 Endive leaves)
2 Apples
2 Bananas
chopped Nuts or Chives
2 tablespoonsful French dressing

Wash and dry green leaves and break up into 3 or 4 pieces; grate the apple, including the skin, and immediately combine with French dressing to prevent discoloration; slice bananas. Using the leaves as a base, divide the bananas and dressed apple between individual dishes, and garnish with chopped nuts or chives.

PEACH AND CUCUMBER

This salad is best made with fresh peaches, but tinned may be used.

$\frac{1}{2}$ Cucumber
$\frac{1}{2}$ Peach per person
4 oz. (115g) sour Cream
1 teaspoonful chopped fresh Mint
1 dessertspoonful soft Brown Sugar

Thinly slice the cucumber and sprinkle with brown sugar; stir mint into sour cream and spoon over sliced cucumber; slice the peach halves (having stoned and skinned them if using fresh peaches) and add to mixture. Divide into glasses or bowls, and serve chilled.

TOMATO AND GREEN PEPPER

4 good-sized Tomatoes
1 large Green Pepper
1 tablespoonful soft Brown Sugar
$\frac{1}{2}$ teaspoonful Italian seasoning Herbs

Scald and skin the tomatoes (i.e., immerse them in boiling water for one minute, remove and skin), slice thinly onto a dish and sprinkle with sugar and Italian seasoning; core and de-seed pepper, and with a very sharp knife cut into thin strips. Arrange the pepper strips in criss-cross pattern over the tomatoes, and serve on individual dishes.

ORANGE, GRAPE AND WATERCRESS

3 Oranges or 4 Satsumas
1 bunch of Watercress
6 oz. (170g) Grapes (black or white)
3 tablespoonsful Lemon French dressing

Peel oranges and divide into segments, and halve; halve grapes and remove pips. Mix oranges and grapes together in the dressing. Divide between individual dishes and garnish with watercress.

CREAM CHEESE, CELERY AND SUNFLOWER SEEDS

8 oz. (230g) Cream Cheese
1 head Celery
2 oz. (60g) Sunflower Seeds
Freshly ground Black Pepper and Sea Salt

Break up cream cheese with a little milk and whip slightly adding pepper and salt. Wash and dry celery, discarding the tough sticks, and chop thinly. Mix chopped celery with cream cheese and add sunflower seeds. Divide into bowls.

STUFFED TOMATOES

4 large Tomatoes
4 level tablespoonsful ground Almonds
$\frac{1}{2}$ teaspoonful Oregano
1 teaspoonful Parmesan Cheese
Lettuce leaves or Cress

Slice off tops of tomatoes, and scoop out seeds and cores into a small basin. In another basin mix the almonds, oregano and cheese, and add the tomato pulp gradually. The mixture needs to be firm for stuffing, so some of the tomato pulp may have to be left if the mixture begins to get too soft. Stuff the tomato cases and serve on lettuce leaves or mustard and cress.

STUFFED PRUNES

3 to 4 large Prunes per person
2 large Tomatoes
4 oz. (115g) Cottage or Cream Cheese
$\frac{1}{2}$ teaspoonful chopped Mint or Chives
Celery, Chicory or Apple

Wash prunes in hot water and work them between finger and thumb to loosen stone, with a sharp knife make a slit and remove stone with as little flesh adhering to it as possible. Mix cheese with mint or chives and, with a teaspoon, stuff mixture into the prunes. Stick in a stalk of celery, chicory or apple, and place each prune on a slice of tomato.

DRIED APRICOT, PINEAPPLE AND ALMOND

4 oz. (115g) dried Apricots
1 small fresh Pineapple
(or medium tin of Pineapple rings)
2 oz. (60g) blanched Almonds
Olive Oil and Lemon Juice

Wash apricots in hot water and allow to soak for ten minutes to soften; remove, dry and cut in half; peel the pineapple carefully and slice and chop on a large shallow dish to retain the juice. Add the apricots, a tablespoonful of olive oil and half a tablespoonful of lemon juice and mix together. Coarsely chop almonds. Divide the mixture between individual dishes and generously garnish with the almonds.

APPLE, BANANA AND GINGER

3 large Apples
2 Bananas
2 to 3 pieces stem Ginger
Juice of a Lemon
Honey
Lettuce, Endive or Cress

Core and dice the apples. Mix teaspoonful honey with lemon juice and toss in diced apple and stir. Peel, slice and dice the bananas, slice and finely chop the stemmed ginger. Mix all together thoroughly and serve on base of lettuce leaves, endive or cress.

BRUSSELS SPROUT SALAD

8 oz. (230g) Brussels Sprouts
1 large Carrot
1 Apple
1 tablespoonful Currants
2 hard-boiled Eggs
Lemon Juice
Yogurt (natural)

Wash sprouts and remove any coarse leaves, dry and chop finely; grate carrot and apple (including skin) and sprinkle with lemon juice. Mix all together in a basin with 2 tablespoonsful natural yogurt. Divide between individual dishes and decorate with currants and peeled and quartered egg.

KEBABS (for Parties or Barbecues) – 1

1 cupful reconstituted Soya Meat (chunky variety)
6 large Prunes
12 stuffed Green Olives
2 sticks Celery

Wash prunes in hot water and work them between finger and thumb to loosen stone, then halve; halve stuffed olives and cut celery into 12 pieces. Divide between 6 kebab sticks or skewers, alternating the ingredients so that there are two sets on each stick.

KEBABS (for Parties or Barbecues) – 2

$\frac{1}{2}$ Green Pepper
2 cupsful small Mushrooms
1 cupful dried Apricots
$\frac{1}{2}$ Cucumber or 2 Courgettes
6 hard-boiled Eggs or Nutmeat Sausages
4 Tomatoes

Sauce:
1 teaspoonful French Mustard
1 tablespoonful Apple Jelly (Mint, Redcurrant or Quince)
1 tablespoonful Lemon Juice or Cider Vinegar
1 tablespoonful Tomato *Purée* or Concentrate
1 teaspoonful soft Brown Sugar
6 tablespoonsful Olive Oil
Sea Salt and freshly ground Black Pepper

Core and de-seed green pepper and cut into 'matchsticks'; halve mushrooms, cover with boiling water, leave 5 minutes and drain. Soak apricots in hot water and drain; slice cucumber or courgettes; quarter the eggs, or cut nutmeat into chunks; quarter tomatoes. Spike pieces of all these onto skewers and brush well with the sauce (made by blending the above ingredients together). Grill or cook over a charcoal fire.

BARBECUE DIPS

French Mustard Dip

> 2 portions Cream Cheese
> 2 to 3 tablespoonsful Milk
> 1 tablespoonsful French Mustard
> 1 teaspoonful soft Brown Sugar

Soften the cheeses with the milk and beat lightly; add the sugar and mustard and mix well.

Tomato and Yeast Extract Dip

> 3 portions Cream cheese
> $\frac{1}{2}$ teaspoonful Yeast Extract
> 1 tablespoonful Tomato Concentrate
> 1 teaspoonful soft Brown Sugar

Mix all together in a blender. The cheeses may need a little milk to soften them to a really creamy consistency.

Curry Dip

> $\frac{1}{2}$ cupful Mayonnaise
> $\frac{1}{2}$ cupful natural Yogurt
> 1 teaspoonful Curry Powder
> $\frac{1}{2}$ teaspoonful Turmeric
> $\frac{1}{4}$ teaspoonful Ginger
> $\frac{1}{4}$ teaspoonful Paprika

Mix together and chill for one hour.

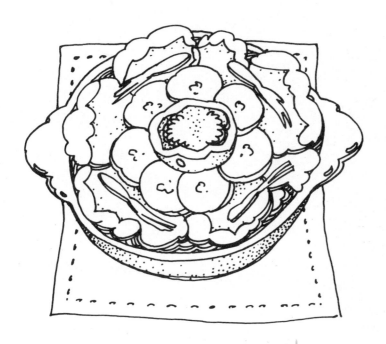

GREEN and SIDE SALADS

On the Continent and in America side salads feature on the menu far more than they do here. However the idea is spreading in Britain for there is nothing nicer than a crisp green salad – well tossed and appetizing – to accompany a hot meal. The contrast in hot and cold, in crisp and soft texture, and in colour, aids digestion and the bonus of vitamins and undiminished mineral salts makes the meal more health-giving.

MIXED VEGETABLE SIDE SALAD

1 cupful finely chopped Celery
1 Carrot
2 small Onions
1 cupful finely shredded Cabbage
3 Tomatoes
$\frac{1}{4}$ Cucumber
French dressing

Grate carrot; chop onions; skin and slice tomatoes and slice cucumber. Combine all ingredients in a bowl and add French dressing. Mix and serve.

LES CRUDITES

1 large Carrot
1 raw Beetroot
1 Turnip
8 to 12 Radishes
$\frac{1}{4}$ Cucumber
Olive Oil and Sea Salt

Wash, peel and grate carrot, beetroot and turnip, and arrange on a large plate in heaps separating them with radishes. Slice cucumber and arrange round edge of plate, and pour on salted olive oil.

GREEK SALAD

1 Cucumber (smaller, rough kind if possible)
6 large Tomatoes
1 clove of Garlic
6 oz. (170g) Black Olives
6 oz. (170g) white goat's milk Cheese
(can be substituted by white Stilton)
4 to 6 tablespoonsful Olive Oil
1 tablespoonful Tarragon Vinegar

Slice cucumber and tomatoes; finely chop garlic and sprinkle over cucumber and tomatoes; add olives and crumble cheese over them; spoon on the olive oil and sprinkle with vinegar. Serve with vegetable casserole or fish dishes.

GREEN SALAD BOWL

$\frac{1}{2}$ Cos Lettuce
1 cabbage Lettuce
1 piece Chicory
1 bunch of Watercress
$\frac{1}{4}$ Cucumber
1 hard-boiled Egg
1 teaspoonful Parsley (finely chooped)
1 teaspoonful Chives (finely chopped)
French dressing

Tear lettuces into pieces; separate chicory leaves; wash and dry watercress; slice cucumber; chop up hard-boiled egg. Toss all but the egg, parsley and chives into salad bowl, add French dressing and mix with a wooden spoon. Now sprinkle with chopped egg, and garnish with parsley and chives.

SEAKALE

8 oz. (230g) Seakale
1 small Celeriac
Lettuce leaves
chopped Cashew Nuts

Wash seakale and cut into narrow strips lengthwise; peel and grate celeriac. Arrange lettuce leaves in a bowl, pile the celeriac in the middle and surround with seakale strips. Sprinkle with oil and lemon and top with chopped cashew nuts.

NASTURTIUM

Nasturtium leaves and flowers
Cabbage leaves (heart)
Watercress
Mustard and Cress
Mint and Parsley
French dressing

Wash and well drain all ingredients; chop mint and parsley; toss salad in French dressing. Arrange in bowl and sprinkle with mint and parsley. Top with flowers, which can be eaten.

ARTICHOKE

12 oz. (340g) Jerusalem Artichokes
1 bunch Watercress
$\frac{1}{4}$ Cabbage heart
milled Brazil Nuts
Oil and Lemon Juice
Cream Cheese

Scrub artichokes, grate finely and mix with oil and lemon juice; wash watercress; wash cabbage, drain well and finely shred. Make a centre of artichoke and arrange watercress and cabbage around. Sprinkle with nuts and small cubes of cream cheese.

BROAD BEAN

8 oz. (230g) cold cooked Broad Beans
Salad dressing
2 tablespoonsful chopped Parsley
2 hard-boiled Eggs
Lettuce leaves and Watercress

Combine broad beans in salad dressing and chopped parsley; pile onto a bed of lettuce and watercress and sprinkle with chopped hard-boiled eggs.

ORANGE AND CUCUMBER
(Serves 8)

2 cabbage Lettuce
3 Oranges
1 small Cucumber
½ Spanish Onion

Dressing:
½ cupful Oil
3 tablespoonsful Cider or White Wine Vinegar
¼ teaspoonful Mustard powder
Sea Salt and freshly ground Black Pepper

Peel and section oranges; thinly slice cucumber and onion, separating rings. Arrange lettuce leaves in a shallow bowl and surround with rings of cucumber and orange slices; top with onion rings. Combine dressing ingredients in blender, or shake well in a screw-top jar, and sprinkle over salad.

EGG, ENDIVE AND CELERIAC

1 Endive
3 hard-boiled Eggs
4 to 6 tablespoonsful grated Celeriac
natural Yogurt
Olive Oil and Lemon dressing

Wash and drain endive, discarding the outer leaves, and arrange in a bowl; mix the grated celeriac with yogurt and spoon onto the endive; slice the eggs and arrange around the edge of the celeriac. Add dressing and serve.

ONION AND WATERCRESS

1 large Spanish Onion
1 bunch Watercress
Radishes for garnish
Cream Cheese/Lemon French dressing

Peel and thinly slice the onion; wash and dry watercress. Arrange sliced onion at bottom of salad bowl, and make a ring of watercress sprigs on top. Decorate with radish slices and top with cream cheese or lemon French dressing.

LETTUCE AND CHICORY

1 head of Lettuce
1 heart of Chicory

Dressing:
2 tablespoonsful Olive Oil (or similar)
1 tablespoonful Lemon Juice (or Cider Vinegar)
1 pinch Garlic Powder

Wash lettuce and chicory, and separate leaves. Mix dressing ingredients. Tear up the lettuce into small pieces, and tear chicory leaves in half lengthwise; put into a bowl and pour over the dressing. Toss salad with wooden servers until well coated, and serve at once.

CARROT SIDE SALAD

2 large Carrots
2 medium Apples
2 sticks Celery
2 tablespoonsful chopped Nuts
2 tablespoonsful French dressing
sprigs of Parsley or Watercress

Coarsely grate carrots and apples; chop celery and mix all together quickly in the dressing to avoid discoloration. Divide into individual dishes, and garnish with chopped nuts and parsley (or watercress).

POOR MAN'S SIDE SALAD

Curly Kale
Bergamot leaves, Mint or Chives
1 Carrot
1 tablespoonful Olive Oil
1 teaspoonful Barbados Sugar
1 dessertspoonful Lemon Juice or Cider Vinegar

Wash, shake and crisp curly kale, allowing 2 to 3 leaves per person; cut carrot into long thin slivers; break up kale into small pieces and toss with carrot slivers and bergamot leaves (mint or chives) in a bowl with olive oil, sugar and lemon juice or cider vinegar.

BRUSSELS SPROUT AND CELERY SIDE SALAD

8 oz. (230g) Brussels Sprouts
1 head of Celery
Oil and Lemon dressing/Cream Cheese dressing

Clean sprouts and celery, drain well and dry. Using a chopping board and sharp kitchen knife chop sprouts and celery together fairly finely; immediately spoon into bowls and pour on enough dressing – approximately 1 dessertspoonful per person – and mix well to coat and seal the cut edges. Serve at once, or put into fridge if there is any delay.

SPINACH

8 oz. (230g) small leaf Spinach
1 Lemon
2 tablespoonsful Oil (Olive, Sunflower, Corn, etc.)
Celery Salt
Chives

Wash, trim and dry spinach. Finely chop chives and make up dressing by adding these to the juice from the lemon, the oil and the celery salt. Tear up the spinach and pour on dressing.

LETTUCE AND HERB

2 large Lettuces
2 tablespoonsful Lemon Juice or Cider Vinegar
6 tablespoonsful Oil
1 tablespoonful finely chopped Chervil
1 tablespoonful finely chopped Chives
1 tablespoonful finely chopped Parsley
1 pinch Sea Salt
$\frac{1}{2}$ teaspoonful Brown Sugar

Wash and dry lettuce; make up the dressing with the other ingredients. Break up the lettuce and toss in the dressing. Serve immediately.

RADISH

2 bunches Radishes
$\frac{1}{2}$ cupful natural Yogurt
Juice from a Lemon
Celery Salt
$\frac{1}{2}$ teaspoonful soft Brown Sugar

Wash radishes and slice thinly into dressing which is made up by mixing together the other ingredients. Serve immediately as radishes will go limp if left in dressing for too long.

PEPPER AND MUSHROOM

2 Green Peppers
4 oz. (115g) Mushrooms
Lemon and Honey dressing

Wash and dry peppers and mushrooms; remove pips and core from peppers and peel mushrooms if preferred. Using chopping board and sharp kitchen knife slice thinly the peppers and mushrooms (stems as well). Mix together in the dressing. *Delicious with nut meats.*

WATERCRESS AND GRAPEFRUIT

2 Grapefruit
2 bunches Watercress
2 Lettuce hearts
½ cupful Olive Oil
½ cupful Tarragon Vinegar

Peel and divide grapefruit into sections; wash, dry and chop watercress and mix with one lettuce heart broken into small pieces. Line salad bowl with second lettuce heart leaves, and add the watercress and lettuce mixture. Cover and chill until needed. Mix grapefruit with olive oil and vinegar and add to the green salad when serving.

FENNEL (Root and Leaf)

1 large Fennel root
½ Webb's Wonder Lettuce
½ cupful finely chopped Fennel leaves
3 Tomatoes
¼ cupful Cider Vinegar
1 pinch of Sea Salt
1 pinch of Garlic Salt
1 pinch of freshly ground Black Pepper
½ cupful Olive Oil

Cut fennel root in half lengthwise and slice thinly across, and thinly slice the tight packed lettuce. Combine the sliced fennel, lettuce and chopped fennel leaves in a salad bowl. Peel and slice tomatoes and add to salad. Combine the rest of the ingredients in a jar and shake well; pour over salad, mix in gently and serve at once.

AUBERGINE

1 large Aubergine
Juice from a Lemon
$\frac{1}{2}$ teaspoonful Sea Salt
1 clove of Garlic
1 tablespoonful chopped Onion
2 tablespoonsful chopped Celery
French dressing
Lettuce; Parsley; Mayonnaise

Peel aubergine, dice and cook in water with lemon juice and garlic and salt for about 5 minutes until barely done. Drain; mix with onions, celery and French dressing. Chill for an hour, and serve on lettuce with mayonnaise and parsley on the side.

KOHL-RABI (Winter Salad)

1 lb 2 oz. ($\frac{1}{2}$kg) Kohl-Rabi
1 Endive
1 large Tomato
Mayonnaise
Oil and Lemon dressing

Steam the kohl-rabi and cool; slice thinly and combine with enough mayonnaise to coat. Serve on a bed of torn up endive tossed in oil and lemon dressing. Garnish with sliced tomato.

VEGETABLE and RICE SALADS

These can be adapted, as can all the others, and be used as an accompaniment to other dishes, or enlarged to be the main course or part of a buffet. The vegetables can be a combination of cooked or raw and this adds to their interest.

For the rice salads it is preferable to use 'brown' rice (which retains some of the bran). Long grain is better for separating out; the round grain is better for puddings. Brown rice takes longer to cook than the ordinary rice – 25 to 35 minutes – but this is worthwhile because brown rice has a better flavour and consistency, and is richer in vitamin B. Rice salads usually include raw and cooked vegetables and should be served with something raw; a tossed green salad, for instance, or tomato salad.

CHICORY, CARROT AND SULTANA

4 heads Chicory
3 large Carrots
2 oz. (60g) Sultanas
Mayonnaise
1 oz. (30g) chopped Walnuts
4 hard-boiled Eggs
Parsley
Lettuce

Slice chicory and grate carrots; rinse sultanas in hot water and drain. Mix all together in a bowl with mayonnaise. Serve on bed of lettuce and garnish with walnuts. Halve the eggs and sprinkle with chopped parsley, and arrange around.

RAW VEGETABLE

1 small Cauliflower
4 oz. (115g) Runner Beans
1 large Carrot
$\frac{1}{4}$ Cucumber
2 small white Turnips
2 tablespoonsful chopped Chives
$\frac{1}{2}$ cupful young Peas
Yogurt or sour Cream, with Sea Salt
    and Black Pepper, as dressing

Divide cauliflower into florets, string and cut runner beans, grate carrot and thinly slice cucumber and turnips. Place small mounds of cauliflower florets in the middle of each plate, and arrange the ingredients around. Garnish with chives.

CAULIFLOWER AND ORANGE

1 small Cauliflower
2 tablespoonsful Lemon Juice
4 Oranges
1 small head Celery
1 bunch Watercress
1 tablespoonful minced
    or finely chopped Onion
French dressing
Cress
4 hard-boiled Eggs

Divide cauliflower into florets, put in a basin and sprinkle lemon juice over; peel oranges and divide into segments, removing any pips and pith; trim and wash celery and cut into 'matchsticks'. Break up watercress into small sprigs and leaves. Mix all with the onion, and toss in simple French dressing made with lemon juice. Serve on individual dishes on nests of cress, and garnish with chopped eggs.

GARDEN VEGETABLE
(Serves 6)

3 cupsful sliced Tomatoes
4 oz. (115g) Spinach
1½ cupsful cooked Green Peas
1½ cupsful cooked and sliced
   Runner or French Beans
1 cupful diced cooked Beetroot
½ cupful thinly sliced Radishes
½ cupful diced boiled Potatoes
2 Lettuce Hearts
1 clove of Garlic
20 stuffed Olives or Black Olives

Dressing:
½ cupful Salad Oil
3 tablespoonsful Lemon Juice
¼ teaspoonful dried Mustard
½ teaspoonful Paprika
½ teaspoonful ground Sea Salt
1 teaspoonful soft Brown Sugar
a grind or two of Black Pepper

Chill all ingredients. Rub salad bowl with garlic; tear lettuce and spinach leaves, the latter very small. Toss into bowl, add other ingredients, and garnish with olives. Put all dressing ingredients into a glass jar with screw-top and shake vigorously until thick and well-blended (or put into blender). Add to salad and serve.

RED CABBAGE

$\frac{1}{2}$ medium sized Red Cabbage
3 slices Onion
1 Carrot
1 bunch Watercress
1 cupful diced Beetroot (cooked)
1 cupful diced cooked Potatoes
2 large Tomatoes
1 cupful cooked and sliced
    French or Runner Beans
strips of Green Pepper for trimming
$\frac{1}{2}$ clove of Garlic
French dressing

Finely chop cabbage and onion; grate carrot; remove stalks from watercress; scald, skin and cut up small the tomatoes. Rub salad bowl with garlic and toss red cabbage into bowl. Toss potatoes in French dressing. Mix them with the other ingredients, and put the entire mixture of ingredients on the cabbage. Garnish with strips of peppers, and serve with French dressing.

LEEK AND TOMATO

8 Tomatoes
3 Leeks
1 Apple
1 tablespoonful Lemon Juice
2 tablespoonsful Olive Oil
1 teaspoonful Barbados Sugar
Sea Salt
Endive leaves or Cress

Scald and skin tomatoes and slice or cut into chunks as preferred. Wash and trim leeks thoroughly, cut lengthwise and then into small pieces and sprinkle with a *little* salt. Dice apple and sprinkle with lemon juice. Whisk remaining ingredients together to make dressing. Mix tomato, leeks and apple together and pour dressing over. Serve on endive leaves or in a nest of cress.

WALNUT, APPLE AND CELERIAC
(Serves 2)

1 Celeriac
2 Apples
Juice of a Lemon
Sprigs of Watercress or Parsley
2 tablespoonsful roughly chopped Walnuts
1 teaspoonsful soft Brown Sugar
3 tablespoonful Olive Oil
$\frac{1}{2}$ teaspoonful Celery Salt

Peel celeriac, but not the apples, and cut both into really thin slices, sprinkling with lemon juice to prevent discoloration. Make a dressing of the oil, salt and sugar. Arrange the mixture on plates with a few sprigs of watercress or parsley to garnish. Top with chopped walnuts. Cover and allow to stand 45 minutes before serving, thus enabling the juices to mingle.

TOMATO AND BLACK OLIVE WITH CHEESE

$\frac{1}{2}$ a head of Endive or Lettuce
8 oz. (230g) Lancashire or Cheshire Cheese
4 oz. (115g) Black Olives
6 Tomatoes
$\frac{1}{2}$ clove of Garlic
soft Brown Sugar
Olive Oil
Lemon Juice

Prepare base of endive or lettuce, using those leaves nearer the heart and toss in oil and lemon and arrange on large dish as a bed for the salad. Scald tomatoes in boiling water for 5 seconds to remove skins. Slice tomatoes on the endive or lettuce and sprinkle with crushed garlic and brown sugar. De-stone and cut up olives, add to salad and squeeze some lemon juice over all. Surround with diced cheese.

HEALTH HYDRO SALAD

Lettuce
1 Tomato
1 heaped tablespoonful each of
    grated Carrot and Beetroot
1 heaped tablespoonful shredded
    Red or Green Cabbage
2 or 3 Spring Onions (in season)
    or slice of Onion
2 or 3 sprigs of watercress
1 dessertspoonful of Raisins
$\frac{1}{2}$ an Apple
1 hard-boiled Egg per person
    or 2 tablespoonsful grated Cheese
1 tablespoonful milled Nuts per person
Oil and Lemon Dressing to taste
    or Yogurt and Honey Dressing

Make nests of lettuce in individual dishes. Quarter tomato and slice apple, dipping in lemon juice to avoid discoloration. Share ingredients amongst dishes and serve with baked (jacket) potato as a main meal.

COURGETTE
(Serves 6 to 8)

2 lb. (900g) Courgettes
3 tablespoonsful Cider Vinegar
$\frac{1}{2}$ teaspoonful Sea Salt
2 teaspoonsful soft Brown Sugar
2 tablespoonsful minced Onion
3 tablespoonsful minced Green Pepper
2 tablespoonsful chopped Parsley
$\frac{1}{2}$ cupful Olive Oil
Lettuce
Watercress

Wash courgettes, cut into thin slices and drop into boiling water and cook for 2 to 3 minutes, then drain well and cool. Mix in a bowl (or shake in a jar) the vinegar, salt, sugar, onion, green pepper, parsley and oil. Beat or shake until blended, and pour over courgettes. Cover and chill for 2 hours – turn over gently one or twice while chilling. When ready, line a salad bowl with the lettuce and watercress and spoon in the courgettes.

KIDNEY BEAN
(Serves 8)

2 tins red Kidney Beans
1 cupful sliced Celery
1 Green Pepper
1 pickled Dill
$\frac{1}{2}$ cupful Olive Oil
$\frac{1}{2}$ cupful Cider Vinegar
4 tablespoonsful chopped Parsley
4 tablespoonsful chopped Onion
$\frac{1}{2}$ clove of Garlic
1 teaspoonful minced Basil
1 teaspoonful minced Tarragon
1 teaspoonful soft Brown Sugar
1 pinch of Sea Salt
Green Salad
Radishes
2 Tomatoes
Black Pepper

Core and seed green pepper and chop finely, mash garlic clove, slice radishes, quarter tomatoes and slice dill. Mix together beans, celery, green pepper and pickle. Chill. Combine olive oil, vinegar, parsley, onion, garlic, basil, tarragon, sugar and salt. Pour over salad mixture and toss together gently. Arrange on green salad and garnish with sliced radishes and tomatoes. Grind black pepper over all before serving.

BROCCOLI

10 oz. (300g) packet frozen Broccoli
$1\frac{1}{2}$ tablespoonsful finely chopped Onion
$\frac{1}{2}$ clove of Garlic
3 tablespoonsful finely chopped Parsley
1 tablespoonful finely chopped Green Pepper
2 tablespoonsful Cider Vinegar
2 tablespoonsful Lemon Juice
2 tablespoonsful Yogurt
$\frac{1}{2}$ cupful Mayonnaise
1 Lettuce
2 Tomatoes

Cook broccoli as directed; drain and chill in covered dish. Mince or mash garlic clove, break lettuce into small pieces and quarter tomatoes. Blend or mix the onion, garlic, parsley, pepper, vinegar, lemon juice, yogurt and mayonnaise. Arrange lettuce on plates, place broccoli on top, and garnish with quartered tomatoes. Stir the dressing before spooning over the salad.

CAULIFLOWER AVOCADO

1 Cauliflower
3 tablespoonsful Wine Vinegar
6 tablespoonsful Olive Oil
1 pinch of Sea Salt and Black Pepper
1 small clove of Garlic
2 Avocados
2 Tomatoes
1 Onion
Lettuce or Endive

Cook cauliflower whole in salted water until tender. (Do not overcook). Chill. Shake together the oil, vinegar, salt and pepper, drop in the garlic and allow to stand, but remove garlic before using the dressing. Peel and mash the avocados; peel and dice tomatoes and mix with chopped onion; add a little salt and whip together until fluffy. Put chilled cauliflower on a dish and garnish with lettuce or endive. Pour oil and vinegar dressing over cauliflower and then top with avocado, tomato mixture.

SALADE DE PROVENCE

1 large Aubergine
½ teaspoonful Lemon Juice
1 teaspoonful finely chopped Onion
1 cupful well-chopped Celery
½ cupful chopped Hazelnuts
Seasoning
1½ tablespoonsful Oil
1 dessertspoonful Cider Vinegar
1 teaspoonful Honey
Lettuce
5 hard-boiled Eggs
8 stuffed Olives

Peel aubergine, cube into medium sized pieces, and cook in a little water to which the lemon juice has been added. Drain and leave to cool. Mix with celery, onion, nuts and seasoning, and add the oil, vinegar and honey, blended together. Serve on a bed of lettuce leaves and decorate with quartered eggs and halved olives.

SALADE NICOISE

4 Tomatoes
½ small Onion
1 Green Pepper
8 Radishes
2 oz. (30g) Black Olives
3 stalks Celery
3 hard-boiled Eggs
3 cooked Potatoes
3 tablespoonsful Olive Oil
2 tablespoonsful Lemon Juice
Sea Salt and Black Pepper
¼ teaspoonful dried Basil

Quarter tomatoes; slice onion; core, seed and slice green pepper; slice radishes; chop celery; quarter hard-boiled eggs; dice potatoes. Mix all vegetables together. Make a dressing of the oil, lemon juice, salt, pepper and basil, and mix into the vegetables. Serve in a bowl after decorating with eggs.

WALDORF SALAD

2 cupsful diced Apples
1 cupful shredded Celery
½ cupful Mayonnaise
2 oz. (60g) roughly chopped Walnuts
Lettuce or Watercress

Mix celery and apples with mayonnaise until well coated. Add most of the walnuts, saving a few to garnish. Serve on bed of lettuce or watercress. Strew with remaining nuts.

RUSSIAN SALAD

3 cold cooked Potatoes
2 cold cooked Carrots
3 small boiled Beetroots
½ cupful toasted and chopped
   Cashew Nuts
1 tablespoonful chopped Parsley
1 tablespoonful chopped Chives
   or Mint
½ tablespoonful Tarragon
Mayonnaise
Green Salad

Cube the potatoes, beetroot, carrots, and mix with the mayonnaise and herbs, taking care not to break the pieces. Pile on a bed of green salad and strew with toasted nuts.

SWEET CORN

8 oz. (30g) Sweet Corn whole kernels (tinned)
4 oz. (115g) Millet
1 large Red Pepper
3 Bananas
1 tablespoonful Lemon Juice
Lettuce
Cress
French dressing with Lemon Juice
Parsley or Chives

Cook millet as directed. Core, seed and thinly slice pepper, thickly slice bananas and quarter the slices. Tear up lettuce leaves, toss in 2 tablespoonsful French dressing and arrange in shallow wooden bowl. Mix sweet corn, red pepper and banana slices and sprinkle with tablespoonful lemon juice. Pile into the middle of the bowl and surround with tufts of cress. Garnish with chopped parsley or chives.

TOMATO AVOCADO

1 large Avocado
2 small Onions
Juice of a Lemon
2 medium sized Tomatoes
1 large Tomato
Heart of Lettuce
1 pinch of Sea Salt and
    Black Pepper
1 pinch of Paprika

Peel, de-stone and mash avocado pulp, finely chop onions and combine with lemon juice in a bowl. Peel and chop the 2 medium sized tomatoes and mix all together with paprika, salt and pepper. Make a bed of lettuce on each place and on it put a thick slice of tomato and pile the avocado mixture on each slice.

WELSH SALAD
(Serves 6)

This is made on a large platter or small tray, the vegetables arranged in rows, and looks very appetizing.

1 Cos Lettuce
1 cupful thinly sliced Celery
1 cupful thinly sliced Leeks
1 cupful thinly sliced Radishes
1 cupful thinly sliced Cucumber
1 cupful finely chopped Green Pepper
3 large Tomatoes
$\frac{1}{2}$ cupful sliced stuffed Olives
3 tablespoonsful Olive Oil
3 tablespoonsful Lemon Juice
1 pinch of Sea Salt
$\frac{1}{2}$ teaspoonful soft Brown Sugar
2 tablespoonsful finely chopped Mint
2 tablespoonsful finely chopped Parsley

Tear lettuce into small pieces and thinly slice the tomatoes. Make a bed of the lettuce, and arrange each vegetable in a row, alternating the colours. Garnish with the olives. Mix parsley, mint, oil, lemon, salt and sugar, and sprinkle over the salad as dressing.

STUFFED TOMATO

6 Tomatoes
$1\frac{1}{2}$ cupsful chopped Pineapple
  (fresh if available)
$\frac{1}{2}$ cupful chopped roasted Peanuts
2 tablespoonsful Lemon French dressing
$\frac{1}{2}$ teaspoonful Sea Salt
Lettuce leaves

Scald and peel tomatoes and cut a slice from top of each; remove pulp and seeds. Chill the tomatoes. Mix together tomato pulp and pineapple, peanuts, dressing and salt. Stuff tomatoes with the mixture. Serve on the lettuce leaves. Overfill the tomatoes as there will be more than required to stuff neatly.

POTATO

6 medium sized Potatoes
1 medium sized Onion
Capers
Parsley and Watercress

Steam potatoes in their jackets and skin and dice while still warm. Stir into a thick mayonnaise, add finely chopped onion and capers to taste. Chill. Serve with sprigs of parsley and watercress.

POTATO AND CUCUMBER
(Serves 6)

2 lb. (1kg) new Potatoes
1 teaspoonful soft Brown Sugar
$\frac{1}{2}$ teaspoonful ground Sea Salt
1 pinch of Mustard Powder
1 pinch of freshly ground Black Pepper
3 tablespoonsful Cider Vinegar
2 teaspoonsful Carraway, Fennel
  or Dill seeds (optional)
1 Cucumber
$\frac{3}{4}$ pt. ($\frac{1}{2}$l) sour Cream
Lettuce
Paprika

Boil potatoes in skins, peel and slice thinly. Mix sugar, salt, pepper, mustard, seeds and vinegar, sour cream and cucumber. Combine with potatoes. Chill. Serve in lettuce-lined bowl and sprinkle with paprika.

CRUNCHY SALAD
(Serves 2)

1 cupful finely shredded White Cabbage
  (or Brussels Sprouts)
1 cupful finely chopped Celery
1 cupful coarsely grated Apple
$\frac{1}{2}$ cupful chopped Watercress
Lettuce leaves
Parsley Sprigs
Radishes or Sesame Seeds
Yogurt Mint dressing

Mix cabbage, celery, apple and watercress together, spoon over the dressing, mix again and turn onto a bed of lettuce leaves. Garnish with radishes or sesame and parsley. Sesame seeds give a delicious nutty flavour and add to the crunchiness.

GRATED CUCUMBER
(Serves 6)

2 Cucumbers
2 cupsful Yogurt
2 tablespoonsful Sultanas
2 tablespoonsful chopped Walnuts
1 Onion
3 Tomatoes
1 pinch of Sea Salt and Black Pepper
$\frac{1}{2}$ teaspoonful dried Mint
   (or 1 teaspoonful fresh)
1 pinch dried Marjoram
Fennel fronds

Grate cucumbers and drain excess juice; soften sultanas in boiling water for 5 minutes; mince or finely chop onion; slice tomatoes; mix cucumber with yogurt and add remaining ingredients. Chill. Serve surrounded by ring of tomato slices and fronds of fennel.

CURRIED RICE

2 cupsful chilled cooked Rice
1 medium sized Green Pepper
$\frac{1}{2}$ tin Red Peppers
2 tablespoonsful Raisins
2 tablespoonsful chopped Parsley
2 tablespoonsful chopped green
　　Onion Shoots
4 tablespoonsful Olive Oil
3 tablespoonsful Cider Vinegar
1 tablespoonsful Lemon Juice
1 clove of Garlic
1 tablespoonful soft Brown Sugar
$\frac{1}{2}$ teaspoonful Curry Powder
Green Salad of Lettuce, Cress
　　and Chicory
2 to 3 Tomatoes

Core, seed and shred green pepper; drain red peppers and cut into strips; mash garlic clove, and quarter tomatoes. Using two forks mix the rice, green pepper, red pepper, raisins, parsley and onion. Chill. Mix oil, vinegar, lemon juice, garlic, sugar and curry powder. Pour over chilled rice salad just before serving and mix well. Serve on the green salad, arranged in shallow bowl, and garnish with tomato quarters.

RED CABBAGE, ONION, AND APPLE

1 lb. (500g) Red Cabbage
2 oz. (60g) Raisins or Sultanas
4 dessert Apples (green skinned)
$\frac{1}{2}$ to 1 Onion, according to size and taste
Honey-Yogurt dressing

Wash cabbage, remove stumpy core, and shred finely with a very sharp knife; chop the apples without peeling; wash raisins in warm water to soften them; finely chop onion. Mix all together, and toss in honey-yogurt dressing.

BLACKBERRY, COCONUT AND RICE

2 cupsful cooked Brown Rice (cold)
2 cupsful fresh Blackberries
$\frac{1}{2}$ cupful desiccated Coconut
$\frac{1}{2}$ cupful chopped Hazelnuts
$\frac{1}{2}$ cupful Milk Powder
1 pinch of Sea Salt
$\frac{2}{3}$ cupful Olive, Sunflower,
  or Corn Oil
2 tablespoonsful Lemon Juice
chopped Parsley
Honey to taste (say 2 tablespoonsful)

Mix the rice, berries, coconut, nuts, and honey in a bowl. Blend the milk powder, salt and 1 tablespoonful honey and, while blending, add oil slowly until mixture thickens. Stir in lemon juice. Fold this cream into the rice and berry mixture. Sprinkle with chopped parsley.

SALADS WITH FRUIT

Although fruit is included – and sometimes predominates – in this section, the recipes are intended for use as savoury courses.

MELON

1 Honeydew Melon
2 to 3 pieces stem Ginger
2 Celery hearts
2 cupsful cooked Green Peas (cold)
2 tablespoonsful Pine Kernels
Juice from a Lemon
Juice from an Orange
1 tablespoonsful chopped Mint

Cut melon in half lengthways and remove seeds, spoon out all the flesh into a mixing bowl and chop fairly small – keeping melon cases to one side. Finely chop the ginger and celery and add to the melon flesh, mixing in the peas and pine kernels. Combine the mint with the orange and lemon juice. Return the mixture to the two halves of melon skin and pour some minted juice over each half.

PEACH AND CREAM CHEESE

4 oz. (115g) Cream Cheese
1 tablespoonful Milk
8 Peach halves (fresh if possible)
Cos Lettuce leaves
Paprika
$\frac{1}{2}$ cupful chopped Nuts

Soften the cheese with the milk, and fill the peach halves with this. Put the filled halves onto lettuce leaves, sprinkle with paprika and chopped nuts, and serve.

APRICOT, APPLE AND GINGER

12 oz. (340g) tin Apricot halves
2 to 3 Apples (as to size)
3 pieces stem Ginger
1 dessertspoonful chopped Mint
2 tablespoonsful Mayonnaise
Lettuce
Watercress
French dressing

Dice apples; finely chop stem ginger. Tear up lettuce and watercress and toss in French dressing. Mix apricots, apple and ginger together in mayonnaise, pile onto lettuce and watercress base, and sprinkle with mint.

PINEAPPLE AND COCONUT

1 cupful cubed Pineapple
1 cupful shredded Coconut
2 cupsful shredded Cabbage
1 cupful Mayonnaise
1 teaspoonful Lemon Juice
Lettuce leaves

Combine all ingredients (except lettuce leaves) and toss gently. Chill, and serve on lettuce base.

GRAPEFRUIT AND PRUNE

$\frac{1}{2}$ Grapefruit per person
4 Prunes per person
Lettuce leaves
Cream

Peel grapefruit whole, and divide into segments, removing all skin. Break segments in half into a mixing bowl. Wash prunes in hot water, roll between finger and thumb to soften, and cut flesh away from stones. Mix the two fruits together and allow to stand for 1 to 2 hours before serving on the lettuce leaves. Top with a teaspoonful of cream.

AVOCADO WITH GRAPEFRUIT AND PRUNE

$\frac{1}{2}$ Avocado per person
1 tablespoonful Grapefruit and Prune
    Salad per person*
Cream Cheese

Halve and de-stone avocados, and pile one tablespoonful of grapefruit and prune salad on top of each half, and top this with the cream cheese.

*See previous recipe.

ORANGE AND OLIVE

4 Spanish Oranges (Blood Oranges if possible)
2 Shallots
8 oz. (230g) Black Olives
2 tablespoonsful Olive Oil
1 pinch Sea Salt
$\frac{1}{2}$ teaspoonful soft Brown Sugar
1 head of Chicory

Peel oranges and slice very thinly; thinly slice shallots and mix with orange; stone and cut in half the olives and add to mixture. Add salt and sugar to the oil, mix, and pour over the salad. Separate the chicory leaves, cut in half across and then into slivers lengthways. Criss-cross these on a plate, and pile the dressed salad over them.

PEAR, GRAPE AND ALMOND
(Serves 6)

3 to 4 ripe fresh Pears
1½ cupsful Black Grapes
2 oz. (60g) Cheese (Edam,
   Gruyere or similar)
3 tablespoonsful blanched, split and
   toasted Almonds
Lemon and Honey dressing
Lettuce

Core and slice pears; de-pip grapes; dice cheese. Arrange lettuce on a tray or large dish, and put the pear slices and grapes on this, either in alternating rows or in a design. Sprinkle with cheese and nuts and add the dressing.

NUTMEAT AND ORANGE

1 tin Nutmeat
4 Spring Onions
2 Celery Stalks
1 sprig of Rosemary
4 small Oranges or Clementines
Olive Oil
Wine Vinegar
Lettuce leaves
Black Olives

Dice the nutmeat; finely chop the onions and celery; peel and separate the oranges. Line a glass bowl or plate with lettuce leaves. Combine the nutmeat, onions and celery with a dressing of 1 dessertspoonful olive oil, 2 dessertspoonsful lemon juice, and add herbs and seasoning. Mix everything well, add the orange segments and put all in the bowl and decorate with the black olives.

GRAPEFRUIT, CHERRY AND RASPBERRY

1 Grapefruit
1 lb. (450g) Black Cherries
1 lb. (450g) Raspberries
4 0z. (115g) finely chopped Nuts
1 head of Lettuce
Lemon and Honey dressing
soft Brown Sugar

Divide grapefruit into segments, cut up, cover with soft brown sugar and allow to stand. Save some cherries for decoration and de-stone remainder. Line salad bowl or individual plates with lettuce leaves. Arrange grapefruit, cherries and raspberries, and cover with the lemon and honey dressing. Sprinkle with chopped nuts and top with 'saved' cherries.

MIXED FRUIT

1 cupful Pineapple cubes (preferably fresh)
3 Bananas
2 Apples
1 Grapefruit
1 Melon
4 pieces Chicory
Watercress
Lemon and Honey dressing
soft Brown Sugar

Slice bananas; dice apples; peel grapefruit, divide into segments and dip in brown sugar, slice melon into thin wedges. Line salad bowl with chicory and watercress, heap pineapple cubes in centre, pile sliced bananas on top and arrange melon slices and grapefruit segments around. Serve with lemon and honey dressing.

PEAR, WALNUT AND CELERY

2 Pears
4 oz. (115g) Walnuts
1 head of Celery
Salad dressing
Parsley
Mustard and Cress/Lettuce
   and Watercress

Wash and dry celery, removing outer sticks (these can be kept for soup or stockpot) and chop up; finely chop parsley; peel, core and dice pears and put into a bowl with 2 teaspoonsful salad cream; coarsely chop the walnuts. Stir all together, gently adding more salad cream. Serve on a bed of green salad and sprinkle generously with chopped parsley.

PINEAPPLE, CHEESE AND RAISIN

1 fresh ripe Pineapple
4 oz. (115g) Cottage Cheese
2 oz. (60g) toasted Almonds or Cashews
1 heaped tablespoonful Raisins
Lettuce
Watercress

Peel pineapple, cut in half lengthwise and remove central core leaving a furrow; soak raisins in hot water for five minutes and drain; combine cheese, nuts and raisins and pack into the pineapple furrows. Put pineapple halves back together (tie with string if necessary) and chill in fridge for 1½ to 2 hours. When chilled, slice onto a dish of lettuce and watercress.

ORANGE AND BANANA

1 Orange per person
1 Banana per person
1 oz. (30g) Nuts per person
Whipped Cream
1 bunch Watercress
Lemon and Honey dressing

Peel oranges and slice across very thinly; peel bananas and slice thinly; wash and dry watercress and break into small sprigs. Line salad bowl with the sprigs of watercress, add a layer of orange slices, followed in turn by the banana and the chopped nuts. Repeat all four layers again, and top with a few watercress sprigs and small heaps of whipped cream. Chill. Add lemon and honey dressing and serve.

LUXURY MELON AND CHERRY
(Serves 6)

1 Webb's or Cos Lettuce
1 medium Cantaloupe Melon
1 small Pineapple
1 Avocado
$1\frac{1}{2}$ cupsful tinned Cherries
   (morello or black)
1 pinch of Sea Salt
Juice of a Lemon
2 tablespoonsful Sesame Seeds
1 small carton of natural Yogurt

Line salad bowl with lettuce leaves and tear up remainder to form base. Peel melon and pineapple and cut into chunks; peel and slice avocado. Lightly mix the melon, pineapple, avocado, cherries, salt and lemon juice. Pile in the bowl and chill. Mix the sesame seeds (lightly toasted) with the yogurt, add a pinch or two of salt and pepper and use as a dressing.

CHICORY, RAISINS AND APPLE

2 to 3 pieces of Chicory
 (as to size)
2 to 4 tablespoonsful Raisins or
 Sultanas
3 Apples
1 small carton of natural Yogurt
1 Tomato

Wash and dry raisins; slice tomato; grate apples including skin, combine immediately with yogurt, add raisins and mix. *Either*: separate chicory into leaves, pile about 2 tablespoonsful apple mix onto individual plates, arrange leaves to stick out like sunrays and top with slices of tomato. *Or*: keep chicory whole, slice thinly, and add to mixture, dividing onto individual plates and top with tomato slices.

CELERY AND BANANA

1 head of Celery
1 Banana
a few Walnuts
1 tablespoonful Honey
1 tablespoonful Lemon Juice
2 tablespoonsful Top Milk (or
 Single Cream)

Clean celery, then shred or chop it finely and add the lemon juice. Mash the banana and mix well with the celery. Beat the milk (or cream) and honey and add to the mixture. Decorate with walnuts. Can be served either sweet or savoury – as a sweet, just as it is, in sundae glasses – as a savoury, on lettuce leaves and a little grated cheese added.

MOULDED and ASPIC SALADS

Gelatin or agar can be used in these; a little clarity is lost with
the latter, but nutrition is gained in mineral salts, iodine, etc.
This type of salad looks more festive, more important, and is
not at all difficult to make. Fruit and vegetables are utilized
and the different shapes make the salads appear very
appetizing. Ring moulds are particularly useful as they can
accommodate so many varieties of fillings.

MIXED VEGETABLES AND CHEESE IN ASPIC

8 oz. (230g) pack frozen macedoine of Vegetables
2 small Cottage Cheeses
1 pint Vegetable Stock
1 teaspoonful Yeast Extract
2 level teaspoonsful Agar
Lettuce
1 bunch Watercress
3 Tomatoes
4 hard-boiled Eggs
Mayonnaise

Cook vegetables as directed and drain. Dissolve yeast extract in vegetable stock, bring to boil and add the agar, sprinkling it in and stirring at the same time. Boil for 2 to 3 minutes, add vegetables and stir well together. Beat the cheeses until creamy, and stir into the cooling mixture. Spoon into a rinsed-out quart jelly mould, and allow to set for 2 hours. Turn out onto a bed of lettuce, surround with rings of sliced tomatoes, watercress and halved hard-boiled eggs. Spoon mayonnaise over eggs.

PEACH SALAD IN JELLY

4 fresh Peaches
1 thick slice Pineapple
$\frac{1}{2}$ Grapefruit
1 small tin 4 oz. (115g) Black Cherries (stoned)
1 packet Lemon or Lime flavoured Jelly
Whipped Cream
Lettuce
soft Brown Sugar

Skin and slice peaches, cube pineapple; divide grapefruit into segments. Sprinkle grapefruit with soft brown sugar and allow to stand. Make jelly and allow to cool. Mix the sliced peaches, pineapple cubes and grapefruit into the jelly and pour into rinsed mould. Chill until set, then turn out onto a bed of tossed lettuce. Decorate with cherries and serve with whipped cream.

TOMATO ASPIC
(Serves 8)

2 tablespoonsful chopped Celery
1 tablespoonful chopped Onion
1 pinch of Sea Salt and Black Pepper
1 dessertspoonful soft Brown Sugar
$\frac{1}{2}$ teaspoonful Basil
1 tablespoonful Cider Vinegar
1 crushed Bay Leaf
2 cupsful Tomato Juice
2 teaspoonsful Agar
1 cupful Mayonnaise

Cook the celery, seasonings and herbs in the tomato juice until soft; sprinkle on the agar and stir while boiling for 3 minutes. Pour into a ring mould or an ordinary mould and chill until set. If a ring mould is used, turn out onto a plate and fill centre with cottage cheese or eggs in mayonnaise. Surround with watercress. If an ordinary mould is used, turn out onto a bed of lettuce and surround with halved hard-boiled eggs, garnished with parsley.

CREAM CHEESE AND STRAWBERRY RING
(Serves 8)

1 packet Strawberry Jelly
6 oz. (170g) Cream Cheese
4 tablespoonsful Single Cream
1 pinch of Sea Salt
2 oz. (60g) Hazelnuts
1 lb. (450g) Strawberries

Finely chop the hazelnuts. Dissolve jelly in hot water (about $\frac{3}{4}$ pint) and pour a layer into a $1\frac{1}{2}$ quart ring mould. Chill until firm, and chill remaining jelly until it is thickening. In the meantime blend cream, cheese, salt and nuts and shape into small balls. Hull the strawberries and choose the best to go into the ring. Put these and the cheese balls alternately into the ring, pour the remaining cooled jelly over them and chill until completely set. Turn out onto a dish and garnish with any strawberries left over.

JELLIED GAZPACHO SALAD

2 level teaspoonsful Agar
1 tumblerful Tomato Juice
1 large Tomato
2 tablespoonsful Cider Vinegar
$\frac{1}{2}$ Cucumber
$\frac{1}{4}$ teaspoonful crushed Garlic
1 Green Pepper
2 tablespoonsful chopped Onion
1 pinch of Sea Salt and Black Pepper
1 Lettuce
1 piece of Chicory
Mayonnaise or Yogurt dressing

Chop cucumber; core, de-seed and finely chop green pepper. Heat tomato juice and sprinkle in the agar while stirring; boil for 3 minutes, stirring all the time. Scald and skin the tomato, chop it roughly and add it to the hot but cooling tomato and agar, plus the vinegar, green pepper, garlic, cucumber, onion and seasonings. Pour into a rinsed quart mould, and chill until firm. Turn out onto a bed of lettuce and chicory leaves. Serve with mayonnaise or yogurt dressing.

PINEAPPLE CHEESE MOULD
(Serves 6)

$2\frac{1}{2}$ level teaspoonsful Agar
1 tin crushed Pineapple
3 tablespoonsful Lemon Juice
3 tablespoonsful soft Brown Sugar
6 oz. (170g) Cheddar Cheese
1 cupful Double Cream
Lettuce leaves
1 Carrot

Grate cheese and carrot; whip cream. Drain off pineapple juice and heat, dissolving the agar in this and stirring well. Add a little of the pineapple and boil for 3 minutes. Add the rest of the pineapple and heat through, but do not boil again. Remove from heat and add lemon juice and sugar. Chill until beginning to thicken and fold in the cheese and cream. Pour into a rinsed mould and chill until completely set. Serve on lettuce leaves and surround by grated carrot.

GRAPEFRUIT AND AVOCADO JELLY
(Serves 6)

1 packet Lime Jelly
½ cupful Grapefruit Juice
2 Grapefruits
1 Avocado
1 teaspoonful Lemon Juice
½ cupful chopped Celery
Lettuce leaves
3 Tomatoes

Make jelly with less water than specified so that – including the jelly – the volume is ¾ pint. Stir to dissolve and add grapefruit juice. Chill until beginning to thicken. Peel grapefruit and divide segments, peel and slice avocado and sprinkle with lemon juice. Mix the grapefruit, avocado and celery into the jelly, pour into a mould and chill. When set turn out onto a plate of lettuce leaves and surround with rings of tomato. *Minty yogurt dressing goes well with this.*

BLENDED SALADS

These are a boon for the very young, the old, or anyone with chewing or digestive difficulties. They can be served with a variety of proteins, such as cottage or cream cheese, milled nuts, hard boiled or scrambled egg, or minced cold meats or poultry. They should be mixed just before serving, so that valuable vitamins do not oxidize or evaporate. They cannot be too highly praised for introducing all the goodness of salads, without the bulk of cellulose. It might be said that the appearance of these blended salads is rather dull, but by adding bright garnishes, and serving them in attractive bowls or glasses, this can be overcome – it is the food-value that counts. The recipes are for one person, unless otherwise stated.

ORANGE BLEND

2 Tomatoes
1 Orange
2 tablespoonsful Lemon Juice
1 heaped teaspoonful Honey
2 sticks Celery
2 Lettuce leaves
1 to 2 tablespoonsful Sunflower
    Seed Oil
1 heaped teaspoonful powdered
    Brewer's Yeast
Parsley or Mint or milled Nuts

Scald and skin tomatoes; peel and separate orange; cut up celery sticks. Put lemon juice, tomatoes, and orange into blender and whizz for a few seconds. Add celery and lettuce, and whizz again. Finally, add the honey, oil and yeast, and give another whizz, and serve in sundae glasses or bowls. Garnish with finely chopped parsley or mint or finely milled nuts.

BANANA BLEND

2 tablespoonsful Apple Juice
2 ripe Bananas
$\frac{1}{2}$ Apple
$\frac{1}{2}$ bunch Watercress
1 small Carrot
3 tablespoonsful natural Yogurt
Mint or milled Nuts

Slice bananas; chop apple; grate carrot, put juice, yogurt, bananas and apple in blender, whizz for a few seconds, add carrot and watercress, whizz again until smooth. Serve in bowls, and garnish with chopped mint or milled nuts.

STRAWBERRY AND WATERCRESS
(Serves 2)

1 punnet Strawberries
1 bunch cleaned Watercress
1 carton natural Yogurt
Cottage Cheese

Start with strawberries in the blender, then add watercress by degrees, possibly adding a little yogurt if too stiff. Serve with cottage cheese.

PINEAPPLE AND LETTUCE
(Serves 2)

$\frac{1}{2}$ fresh Pineapple (tinned
   pulp will do)
$\frac{1}{2}$ Lettuce
2 tablespoonsful Apple Juice

Put juice and chopped pineapple in blender and whizz, then add as much lettuce as can be absorbed without the mixture getting too stiff.

TVP BASED SALADS

TVP stands for Textured Vegetable Protein, which is a vegetarian alternative to meat, made largely from soyabeans. In reconstituted form it has a texture similar to meat, and weight for weight it is just as high in protein, but with none of the toxic factors which exist in the flesh from animals fed 'scientifically' and slaughtered in fear.

TVP is available in dried form, either in chunks or mince, and the dried 'meat' has to be re-hydrated (or reconstituted) in flavoured stock before serving. It offers an interesting dimension to vegetarian salads.

CHUNKY TVP AND APPLE

4 oz. (115g) chunky TVP (ham flavour)
3 eating Apples
Oil and Lemon dressing
Lettuce leaves
4 Tomatoes

Reconstitute the TVP chunks in savoury stock as directed, and cool. Core, peel and dice apples, toss in oil and lemon dressing, and mix with TVP. Arrange on lettuce leaves and decorate with quartered tomatoes.

GRATED SALAD WITH TVP

2 Carrots
1 Beetroot (raw)
1 Apple
1 tablespoonful Lemon Juice
2 oz. (60g) minced TVP
    (natural flavour)
$\frac{1}{2}$ teacupful Tomato Juice
Mustard and Cress
4 hard-boiled Eggs

Simmer TVP in tomato juice for 5 minutes and allow to cool. Grate carrots, beetroot and apple, and keep each item separate. Mix grated apple with lemon juice to prevent browning. Arrange on plates with spoonful of TVP in centre, surrounded by heaps of grated carrot, beetroot and apple, and framed in mustard and cress and sliced hard-boiled eggs.

COLE SLAW WITH TVP
(Serves 6)

$\frac{1}{4}$ White Cabbage
1 Onion
1 Carrot
2 oz. (60g) TVP mince
　　(natural or ham flavour)
Garlic Salt
Oil and Lemon dressing
$\frac{1}{2}$ teacupful Savoury Stock
　　or Yeast Extract

Soak the TVP in the stock for 15 minutes, stirring once or twice. Finely shred white cabbage, finely chop onion, and grate carrot. Combine all ingredients together. Add oil and lemon dressing, and serve.

CELERY, BEETROOT AND TVP

2 medium-sized Beetroots
best part of head of Celery
4 oz. (115g) chunky TVP
Mayonnaise *(see page 00)*
Watercress

Cook, skin and dice the beetroots, and cut up the celery to similar size. Reconstitute the TVP chunks in savoury vegetable stock and cool. Mix all together in the mayonnaise, and serve in mounds, with watercress surrounding.

TVP AND MUSHROOM
(Serves 2)

$\frac{1}{2}$ cupful Onion
4 oz. (115g) Mushrooms
2 tablespoonsful Parsley
1 breakfast cupful hydrated TVP mince

The TVP is best re-hydrated in water flavoured with yeast extract. Chop onion and mushrooms, add to TVP mince, sprinkle with chopped parsley and serve hot or cold with salad.

TVP AND POTATO CAKES
(makes 6 to 8 according to size)

1 small Onion
1 tablespoonful chopped Parsley
6 oz. (170g) cold mashed Potato
Sea Salt and Black Pepper to taste
1 oz. (30g) Vegetable Fat or Olive Oil

Reconstitute TVP mince in water flavoured with yeast extract. Slice onion and fry gently in the oil until cooked. Remove from heat and combine with the TVP mince, the chopped parsley and the potato. Shape into cakes, dust with flour and fry for 2-3 minutes each side. Drain on kitchen paper. Serve hot with green vegetables or cold salad.

Note: 3 oz. (90g) chopped mushrooms could be substituted for the onion, fried in the same way.

TVP GALANTINE
(Serves 6 to 8)

2 cupsful TVP mince
1 cupful Tomato Juice
1 cupful Brown Rice
2 tablespoonsful Millet Flakes
$\frac{1}{2}$ cupful Vegetable Stock
$\frac{1}{4}$ teaspoonful Tarragon (or Mint)
1 medium-sized Onion
$\frac{1}{2}$ teaspoonful Garlic Salt
2 tablespoonsful chopped Parsley
3 tablespoonsful chopped Nuts
1 Egg

Reconstitute TVP and simmer for 3-5 minutes in the tomato juice. Finely chop onion, cook rice and lightly beat egg. Pre-heat oven to 375°F (Gas No 5). In a bowl combine TVP and rice. Soak millet flakes in the stock for 5 minutes then add to TVP mixture. Add remaining ingredients and mix well. Turn into a well oiled loaf tin (approx. 8$\frac{1}{2}$in. x 4$\frac{1}{2}$in. x 2$\frac{1}{2}$in.). Bake for 45-60 minutes. Remove from heat and cool. Turn out, and serve with salad.

TVP ORIENTAL SALAD
(Serves 3)

1 Green Pepper
1 Tomato
2 tablespoonsful Honey
1 teaspoonful Soy Sauce
4 oz. (115g) Mushrooms
1 cupful chunky TVP
1 cupful Vegetable Stock or Tomato Juice
Butter

Seed and slice pepper, and skin and slice tomato. Lightly fry tomato, pepper and mushrooms in a little butter, add the honey and vegetable stock (or tomato juice). Add the TVP as it is. Cook on low heat, stirring fairly frequently for 30-40 minutes. Cool, and serve with sliced tomatoes and chopped herbs to choice.

MACARONI CHEESE WITH TVP

1 cup chunky TVP
2 tablespoonsful vegetable Margarine
2 tablespoonsful Flour (100% wholewheat)
5 oz. (140g) grated Cheese
2 cupsful cooked Macaroni (brown)
1 cupful Milk
$\frac{1}{2}$ teaspoonful Garlic Salt

Reconstitute TVP in two cupsful water and simmer for 30 minutes. Combine margarine, flour, salt, cheese and milk to make a cheese sauce. Mix the macaroni, TVP and sauce, put into greased oven dish and top with grated cheese. Bake for 20-30 minutes at 325°F (Gas No 3). Serve with tomato salad.

TVP VEGETARIAN CUTLETS

2 small raw Beetroots
1 Carrot
2 Onions
2 Eggs
2 tablespoonsful Oil
$\frac{1}{2}$ teacupful Sunflower Seeds
  (milled or ground)
$\frac{1}{2}$ teaspoonful Caraway Seeds (or
  Fennel)
$\frac{1}{2}$ cupful Wheat Germ
$\frac{1}{2}$ teaspoonful Garlic Salt
1 teacupful TVP mince
$\frac{1}{2}$ teacupful Cider

Peel and finely mince the beetroot, carrot and onions. (Strain off any excess liquid and use for soup). Combine this with remaining ingredients and mix well (if mixture is too wet to form into croquettes add more wheat germ). Chill for 30 minutes. Shape into croquettes or patties. Fry in a little oil until browned on both sides. Serve with rice salad.

TVP COARSE PÂTE

1 lb (½kg) Runner Beans (fresh
   in season, frozen or quick dried)
3 tablespoonsful Oil
2 large Onions
1 stick Celery
2 tablespoonsful Walnuts
3 hard-boiled Eggs
Sea Salt and Black Pepper to taste
1 teacupful TVP mince
Lettuce, Tomatoes and
   Watercress (for salad)

Finely chop onions, celery and walnuts. Reconstitute TVP
mince in water flavoured with yeast extract. Cook the beans as
appropriate, but rather undercook. Heat the oil in a pan and
sauté the onions until tender, add celery and TVP and cook for
a further 3 minutes. Mince the beans, onion mixture, walnuts
and eggs coarsely. Pound all together, pack into a basin, and
chill. Season and serve with lettuce, tomatoes and watercress.

CHUNKY TVP, CHEESE AND PINEAPPLE

1 breakfast cupful TVP
1 cupful Cider or Apple Juice
1 cupful Cheese ·
1 cupful crushed Pineapple
Lettuce, Tomato and Onion rings
   (for salad)

Simmer the TVP chunks in the Cider for 20-30 minutes (add
more Cider if necessary). Allow to cool, mix with grated
cheese and pineapple and serve on lettuce leaves surrounded
by alternating slices of tomato and onion rings.

COTTAGE PIE

5 oz. (140g) TVP (1 large cupful)
2 lbs. (1kg) Potatoes
1 large Onion
1 clove Garlic
1 oz. (30g) Vegetable Fat
1 teaspoonful Yeast Extract
1 teacupful Stock
2 tablespoonsful Tomato Purée
Sea Salt and Black Pepper
1 oz. (30g) Flour (100% wholewheat)

Reconstitute TVP in 2 cupsful water with fine-chopped garlic to flavour. Boil and mash potatoes. Slice and fry onion gently in oil for 10 minutes. Stir in flour, brown slightly, then add yeast extract and stock, and stir until it thickens. Stir in purée, salt and pepper, and mix with the TVP. Turn into a pie dish, top with mashed potato and bake in oven at 350°F (Gas No 4) for 40 minutes until golden brown. Serve with side salad.

TVP SAUSAGES

2 breakfast cupsful TVP mince
1 cupful Lima Beans (Haricot or
  Butter Beans would do)
1 teaspoonful Garlic Salt
2 tablespoonsful Flour
  (100% wholewheat)
$\frac{1}{4}$ teaspoonful Sage
$\frac{1}{4}$ teaspoonful Thyme $\Big\}$ powdered
$\frac{1}{4}$ teaspoonful Marjoram
1 Egg
$\frac{2}{3}$ cupful milk
1 cupful Pease Pudding or Mashed
  Potato
very fine Breadcrumbs or
  medium Oatmeal

Reconstitute TVP mince in water flavoured with yeast extract. Pre-heat oven to 500°F (Gas No 9). Gently cook TVP in water flavoured with yeast extract until all liquid is absorbed. Cook beans and press through a sieve; combine with the pease pudding, herbs and TVP. Mix well and shape into sausages. Combine milk and egg; dip sausages in this, and then in the breadcrumbs or oatmeal. Put into a shallow roasting pan well oiled with olive oil. Bake until sausages are browned all over – turning during cooking. Serve cold with salad.

MUSHROOM AND TVP QUICHE
(Serves 8)

Pastry:

> 8 oz. (230g) Flour (100%
>   wholewheat)
> 4 oz. (115g) Vegetable Fat or Butter
> ½ teaspoonful Garlic Salt
> Water to mix

Mix pastry in usual way, roll out ¼ in. thick and line a 10in. pie tin.

Filling:

> 4 oz. (115g) Mushrooms
> 1 clove Garlic
> 1 breakfast cupful TVP
> 3 Eggs
> 1 breakfast cupful Milk
> Sea Salt and Black Pepper to taste
> Olive Oil

Reconstitute the TVP as directed on packet; slice mushrooms and finely chop garlic. Fry the mushrooms and garlic in a little olive oil for a few minutes, then add TVP. Allow to cool a little – spread over pastry and pour beaten egg and milk over. Bake in hot oven to start with: 425°F (Gas No 7) for 15 minutes, then reduce to 375°F (Gas No 5) for 20 minutes. Serve hot or cold with mixed salad.

RATATOUILLE WITH TVP MINCE

1 small Onion
1 Pepper
1 large Courgette (or $\frac{1}{2}$ Cucumber)
1 small Aubergine
1 clove Garlic
2 Tomatoes
1 breakfast cupful TVP mince
$\frac{1}{3}$ cupful Oil
2 tablespoonsful Flour (100%
    wholewheat)

Seed and slice pepper; chop onion and garlic; slice courgette or cucumber; peel and slice aubergine; skin and chop tomatoes. Sprinkle the aubergine with sea salt and leave to stand. Heat the oil in a thick pan and *sauté* the onion and garlic until tender but not browned. Toss the courgette slices (or cucumber) in $\frac{1}{2}$ the flour and add to the pan. Rinse the aubergine slices, dry and toss in remaining flour, add to the pan. Cook over medium heat for 5 minutes. Cover and cook very slowly for 30 minutes. Add the pepper, tomatoes and TVP and cook uncovered until vegetables are tender and all liquid evaporated. Serve hot or cold, garnished with olives.

RISOTTO WITH CHUNKY TVP

8 oz. (230g) long grain Rice
  (brown for preference)
1 Spanish Onion
2 oz. (60g) Butter or Vegetable Fat
1 pint ($\frac{1}{2}$ litre) Vegetable Stock
8 oz. (230g) chunky TVP
3 sticks Celery
Parmesan Cheese

Reconstitute TVP as directed on packet, finely chop onion, finely slice celery. Melt 2 oz. (60g) butter or vegetable fat in a deep pan; add chopped onion and cook gently until transparent. Now add rice and cook over low heat stirring with a wooden spoon; after 2 minutes add hot stock. Continue cooking, stirring at times, until rice is cooked (15-25 minutes). By this time the stock should be absorbed, add TVP and finely sliced celery and cook for a few minutes more, stirring frequently. Serve sprinkled with parmesan cheese. Delicious cold with salad.

VEGETABLE CURRY AND TVP

6 oz. (170g) TVP
1 medium Onion
1 eating Apple
1 tablespoonful Tomato Purée
$\frac{1}{2}$ teaspoonful Garlic Salt
1 teaspoonful Curry Powder
1 oz. (30g) Sultanas
1 oz. (30g) Flour (100%
 wholewheat)
2 oz. (60g) Butter
6 oz. (170g) long grain Rice
 (brown)
1 cupful Vegetable Stock

Thinly slice onion, chop apple and reconstitute TVP (see directions on packet). Melt butter in a saucepan, and fry onion until soft, add chopped apple and fry gently for a few minutes. Stir in tomato purée, sugar, salt, curry powder and flour and blend well together. Add stock and bring to the boil, stirring all the time until the sauce thickens. Add TVP and sultanas and simmer gently for 10 minutes. Meanwhile prepare rice by tipping it into boiling water and cooking for 20-25 minutes or until soft. Drain and rinse under hot water. Drain again. Serve curry on a bed of rice, or mix curry and rice together, cool and serve with salad.

SALAD DRESSINGS

It is more satisfactory to make your own salad dressings, chiefly because the condiments can be controlled (most proprietary brands having too much seasoning) and the flavours can be varied to suit different needs. The following recipes are very simple, and they will not mask the delicate flavours of your salads.

NATURAL YOGURT

Use straight from the carton, and just spoon over the salad.

HONEY YOGURT

1 small carton natural Yogurt
1 dessertspoonful Clear Honey

Dilute the yogurt with the honey and mix well.

MINTY YOGURT

1 small carton natural Yogurt
1 teaspoonful Lemon Juice
1 dessertspoonful Barbados Sugar
1 teaspoonful chopped Mint

Mix well together.

WATERCRESS YOGURT

1 small carton natural Yogurt
1 teaspoonful Lemon Juice or
   Cider Vinegar
1 teaspoonful Clear Honey
1 teaspoonful Olive Oil
1 heaped tablespoonful chopped
   Watercress

Mix well together.

NUTTY YOGURT

1 small carton natural Yogurt
1 tablespoonful Clear Honey
1 heaped tablespoonful milled Nuts

Beat all together.

LEMON AND HONEY

2 tablespoonsful Clear Honey
1 tablespoonful Lemon Juice
2 tablespoonsful Olive Oil
  (or other oil)
1 pinch Sea Salt
1 grind of Black Pepper

Blend all together and shake up in a bottle.

HORSERADISH DRESSING

$\frac{1}{2}$ cup whipped Cream
2 hard-boiled Egg Yolks
$\frac{1}{2}$ tablespoonful Lemon Juice
1 tablespoonful Vinegar
2 tablespoonsful grated fresh
  Horseradish
(or 1 tablespoonful dried Horseradish)
1 pinch of Sea Salt and
  Black Pepper
soft Brown Sugar

Put the egg yolks into a basin and mortar-mash with wooden spoon until smooth. Add pepper, salt, sugar and horseradish. Slowly add the lemon juice and vinegar, stirring until the mixture is creamy. Finally fold in the whipped cream gradually.

SOUR CREAM

1 large cupful sour Cream
1 pinch Sea Salt and Black Pepper
1 tablespoonful finely chopped Chives
  (or Onion or Mint)
1 teaspoonful Lemon Juice

Mix lemon juice, chives (or onion or mint), salt and pepper, then add the sour cream.

MAYONNAISE

1 raw Egg Yolk
1 tablespoonful French Mustard
1 pinch of Black Pepper
$\frac{1}{2}$ teaspoonful Sea Salt
$1\frac{1}{2}$ cupsful Olive Oil
$\frac{1}{2}$ tablespoonful Lemon Juice or
   Vinegar

Using blender: mix egg yolk and mustard, add salt and pepper, followed by the olive oil and the lemon juice or vinegar. Using screw-top jar, shake all together vigorously.

BASIC FRENCH DRESSING

$\frac{1}{3}$ cupful Wine or Cider Vinegar
1 pinch of Sea Salt and
   Black Pepper
1 cupful Olive Oil

Mix the vinegar, salt and pepper and stir well. Add olive oil slowly, beating all the time. Store in a bottle and shake well before using.

Note: This dressing can be varied by the addition of herbs such as:

1 clove of Garlic, crushed
1 tablespoonful chopped Parsley
1 tablespoonful chopped Mint
1 tablespoonful chopped Chives
1 teaspoonful dried Mixed Herbs
finely chopped Watercress

but all these should be added freshly and not stored.

JUICY FRENCH DRESSING

1 pinch Sea Salt and Black Pepper
3 teaspoonsful soft Brown Sugar
1 pinch of Mustard Powder
2 tablespoonsful Lemon Juice
2 tablespoonsful Orange Juice
   (or Grapefruit)
$\frac{2}{3}$ cupful of Olive Oil

Mix dry ingredients, add fruit juices and stir well. Pour in oil slowly, stirring all the time.

LEMON FRENCH DRESSING

3 tablespoonsful Lemon Juice
1 pinch of Sea Salt and Black Pepper
$\frac{1}{4}$ teaspoonful soft Brown Sugar
1 pinch Mustard Powder (optional)
$\frac{1}{2}$ cupful of Olive Oil

Mix the lemon juice with all the condiments, add the oil teaspoonful by teaspoonful and stir well. Store in a bottle, and shake well before use.

HALF-FAT CREAM CHEESE DRESSING

$1\frac{1}{2}$ tablespoonsful Lemon Juice
2 oz. (60g) Cream Cheese
2 to 3 teaspoonsful soft Brown Sugar
1 pinch of Sea Salt
1 or 2 pinches of Black Pepper
1 squeeze of Garlic Powder

Blend all together in a liquidizer and use immediately. Particularly useful on salads with fruit or cheese.

INDEX